Caring for your car's bodywork and interior

Also from Veloce Publishing –

Caring for your bicycle – How to maintain & repair your bicycle (Henshaw)
Caring for your car – How to maintain & service your car (Fry)
Caring for your scooter – How to maintain & service your 49cc to 125cc twist & go
  scooter (Fry)
Dogs on wheels – Travelling with your canine companion (Mort)
Electric Cars – The Future is Now! (Linde)
First aid for your car – Your expert guide to common problems & how to fix them (Collins)
How your car works – Your guide to the components & systems of modern cars,
  including hybrid & electric vehicles (Linde)
How your motorcycle works – Your guide to the components & systems of modern motorcycles
  (Henshaw)
Land Rover Series I-III – Your expert guide to common problems & how to fix them
  (Thurman)
Motorcycles – A first-time-buyer's guide (Henshaw)
Motorhomes – A first-time-buyer's guide (Fry)
Pass the MoT test! – How to check & prepare your car for the annual MoT test (Paxton)
Roads with a View – England's greatest views and how to find them by road
  (Corfield)
Roads with a View – Scotland's greatest views and how to find them by road
  (Corfield)
Roads with a View – Wales' greatest views and how to find them by road (Corfield)
Simple fixes for your car – How to do small jobs for yourself and save money (Collins)
Selling your car – How to make your car look great and how to sell it fast (Knight)
The Efficient Driver's Handbook – Your guide to fuel efficient driving techniques and car choice (Moss)
Walking the dog – Motorway walks for drivers and dogs (Rees)
Walking the dog in France – Motorway walks for drivers and dogs (Rees)

www.rac.co.uk
www.veloce.co.uk

This publication has been produced on behalf of RAC by Veloce Publishing Ltd. The views and the opinions expressed by the author are entirely his own, and do not necessarily reflect those of RAC. **Please do not undertake any of the procedures described in this book unless you feel competent to do so, having first read the full instructions.**

First published in April 2012 by Veloce Publishing Limited, Veloce House, Parkway Farm Business Park, Middle Farm Way, Poundbury, Dorchester, Dorset, DT1 3AR, England. ISBN: 978-1-845843-88-5 UPC: 6-36847-04388-9

Fax 01305 250479/e-mail info@veloce.co.uk
web www.veloce.co.uk or www.velocebooks.com.

Made under licence from RAC Motoring Services. The RAC logo is the registered trade mark of RAC Motoring Services.
Readers with ideas for automotive books, or books on other transport or related hobby subjects, are invited to write to the editorial director of Veloce Publishing at the above address.
British Library Cataloguing in Publication Data – A catalogue record for this book is available from the British Library.
Typesetting, design and page make-up all by Veloce Publishing Ltd on Apple Mac.
Printed in India by Replika Press.

Caring for your car's bodywork and interior

Simon Nixon

Contents

Introduction

My name is Simon Nixon. I am a professional car valeter/cleaner, and I've been valeting cars and other vehicles for the past 13 years. I started in the valeting trade when I left school at 16, working at a local garage cleaning cars after they had been serviced, repaired, or prepared for sale on the forecourt.

I worked at that garage for two years before leaving to follow another career path, but I eventually returned to the car trade as a vehicle valeter for a local valeting company.

I stayed at that company for three years before deciding to go it alone and set up my own valeting business, a business that I still operate from home, with my partner Sallyann.

People often ask me for advice on car cleaning, particularly certain aspects of the cleaning process – "How do I clean my wheels?" or "How can I remove bugs from my windscreen/windshield?" It was precisely because

of such questions that I decided to write this guide: I realised that there are many people who enjoy keeping their car clean and fresh for themselves.

What is covered in this book?
This book will show you how to clean your car in a clear step-by-step format, which cleaning products you will need to purchase, and the tools you will need.

Some of these tools you'll almost certainly already own or have access to, and if not, they're readily available from your local car accessory shop and many other outlets.

Why should I clean my car?
Apart from the extra pleasure and comfort we enjoy from driving a nice clean, fresh car (doesn't it feel great to get those admiring looks, and comments?), it also makes financial sense to take care of our cars. Your home aside, your car is usually one of

Cleaning your car yourself offers many benefits.

the costliest purchases you'll make in your lifetime, and as such, you'll want it to be at its best for as long as possible.

Also, when the time comes to replace it for a newer or different model, you'll want to sell or trade it in for the best possible price. We all know that keeping your car mechanically sound with regular maintenance and servicing helps it to retain its value, but keeping your car clean is also very important when it comes to selling or trading it.

I'm selling my car: should I bother cleaning it?

Your car's cleanliness and tidiness can have a significant effect on its selling price, whether you're selling to a dealership or selling privately.

At a dealership, it could mean hundreds of pounds less in your hand if it hasn't been looked after. Before your car can be viewed or put on a forecourt, it will need to be valeted, and this

means paying for a valeting company to prepare the car, and delaying a potential sale while the car is readied for viewing.

If you sell your car privately, a potential buyer will inevitably try offering you less than you're asking if your car is less than clean and shiny, and he or she could even be put off buying your car altogether.

A car that hasn't been kept clean and tidy is not only seen as a less desirable purchase, but will also age quicker, looking worn and tired sooner than it should. A car's carpets, for instance, will wear quicker if not regularly vacuumed.

So, with all that in mind let's get started. In chapter one, I'll run through what you'll need and the preparations you should make for cleaning – then you'll be ready to start washing-off your car.

one
What you will need

There are literally thousands of car care and car cleaning products available today, and if you're not sure what you need, it can be quite daunting when faced with such a huge selection. There are also many different brands, each claiming to be the best and give the ultimate finish for your 'pride and joy.'

Products and brands

So, which do you choose? Well, it's the same rule here as for any other purchase: you get what you pay for. Over the years, I've tried hundreds of different products, equipment, and tools, and – almost always – the above statement holds true. Buy the best you can afford. If you buy cheap or budget products, you'll usually get cheap or budget results.

Throughout this book I'll mostly be using and referring to Autoglym products. This is simply because it has

such an extensive selection of easy-to-use car care products, and gives great results. Autoglym has also been around for many years (which tells me that the products it produces are very good), and is highly regarded in the auto trade. Of course, you don't have to use Autoglym products to follow the steps in this book: you may like to try other brands for yourself. All brands will have equivalent products – just remember that you really do get what you pay for.

Where to buy

All of the cleaning products you'll be using should be readily available at your local car care shop, such as Halfords. Some products can be purchased at your local supermarket, or, if you prefer, you could buy them online (a Google search for car cleaning products will return a huge number of results).

I'll start with a list of essential cleaning products, along with a few optional ones, plus a description of what each one does and how to use it. Then, I'll give you a list of tools that you'll need, some of which you will almost certainly already own, or be able to borrow. You can find a handy checklist of these products at the end of this chapter, too, for convenience when shopping.

Let's start with the products you'll use to prepare your car. As with most things, preparation is the key. If you prepare well, then the job will be easier and the end results better, and it's no different when cleaning your car.

Bodywork shampoo/conditioner
The first product you'll need is a good quality bodywork shampoo/conditioner. Cars pick up lots of contaminants from the road when driven: organic substances such as salt and tree sap, plus inorganic substances such as exhaust fumes and other chemicals from factories, other vehicles, and even from rain. This leaves a thin film of residue, known as traffic film, over the entire vehicle. Bodywork shampoo/conditioner contains a traffic film remover to break down these chemicals and substances, helping to loosen them and making washing easier and more effective.

Regular removal of these contaminates also helps prevent damage to your car's paintwork (such as staining), and significantly helps preserve the finish. It also makes polishing easier and more effective, and extends the life of the polish.

Tar remover
This is the next product you'll need. If you travel through areas with new or recently resurfaced roads, you'll almost certainly have picked up some tar on your bodywork. Even a hot summer day can soften tarmac enough to be picked up as deposits on the lower surfaces of your car's bodywork. Not only do tar spots look unsightly, they can also stain certain types of paint.

Tar remover can be sprayed on, and then wiped off with a soft cloth to remove the dissolved tar, or it can be used with your regular washes. It's quite a versatile cleaner, as it will remove sticky stuff such as that left behind by old windscreen/windshield stickers, or gadgets that have been attached to your dash or other interior surfaces.

Use it to remove oil, grease, silicone, wax, fuel stains around your fuel filler cap, and resinous tree sap deposits from parking your car under trees. Most tar removers can also be used on rubber, synthetic carpets, and upholstery, for the removal of oil-based stains, but **always** check the directions on the container.

Wheel cleaner
Normal washing will remove most of the dirt from your wheels, but won't remove black brake dust deposits. There are several types of wheel cleaner available, but I would recommend a non-acid based cleaner, as regular use of acid-based varieties can start to corrode your expensive alloy wheels if not used precisely as directed on the instructions. Having said that, if your car's wheels have been a little neglected, you may need a stronger cleaner to restore them to their original condition, so an acid-based cleaner will be needed – but make sure you always follow the directions for use.

Tyre dressing
Once your wheels are nice and clean, the last thing you'll want is shabby-looking tyres spoiling the effect, so the application of a good tyre dressing will

leave your tyres looking like new, and complete the overall look.

There are generally two types of tyre dressing: a spray-on 'instant' type, or a foam-type. Both types are sprayed-on and left to dry, but, with the first type, if you'd rather have a light sheen on your tyres, rather than the 'wet look,' then you'll need to wipe off the excess before the product dries completely.

Foam dressings tend to be a little cleaner to use, but with both types I would remove overspray from your wheel rims.

Note: A word of warning here. Due to the slippery nature of tyre dressings, for safety reasons don't use them on any rubber mats inside your car!

Insect/bug remover

An insect or bug remover is essential – particularly during the summer months, when you'll find thousands of insect remains deposited on your car's radiator grille, headlights, backs of door mirrors, and your windscreen/windshield. If you drive at higher speeds, such as on a motorway, you'll have plenty of bugs to clean off, and a bug remover will save you a lot of hard work!

Insect remover can usually be used as an 'instant' cleaner, simply spraying it on the insect-covered area, leaving it for a few seconds to soften the deposits, before wiping them away with a cloth. Alternatively, you can spray the affected area prior to washing your car; the insects will then be removed with the wash. If any remain, another application and a wipe over with your cloth will complete the job.

Plastic and vinyl cleaner

If your car has plastic or vinyl exterior trim, such as the cases of door mirrors, door trims, bumpers, or handles, you'll need a product to clean and protect it.

You can buy spray-on types or gel-types: I recommend the gel for your exterior trim, as it's so much cleaner and easier to apply, and can be applied using a small sponge.

Not only will it clean and revive weathered and faded trim, but will, when used regularly, continue to protect it from everyday contaminates and the fading effects of the sun. The spray-type can be used for your car's interior, on fascias, PVC door and seat panels, plus any other similar areas.

Cabriolet/soft top cleaner

For those of you that own a cabriolet, you'll need to purchase two extra items for taking care of the soft top: fabric hood cleaner and protector/reproofer. These can often be obtained as a kit, containing both products, a case for storing them, and often some sort of sponge or cloth for application. The cleaner removes road contaminates, general dirt, algae, and stains, and it gives a fresh, revived look to your hood, whether it's made from natural or synthetic material.

These cleaners tend to work better on a damp roof, but **don't** use a pressure washer, as this can mark the hood. After cleaning, you'll need to use the protector/reproofer to protect the hood from dirt and absorption of water. A vinyl roof can be cleaned with an interior shampoo, and then protected with the vinyl trim spray or gel.

Glass polish

Next is glass polish. Look for one that doesn't contain wax or silicone, as these mark rubber and vinyl trim and can cause your windows to smear in wet weather. But, silicone- and wax-free or not, for safety reasons I would never recommend polishing the outside of your windscreen/windshield. All other windows, and of course your mirrors, inside and out can be polished. You can also buy spray glass cleaners for a quick clean and sparkle: these are great if you carry a dog in your car – they can make your windows very messy with their wet noses! Both the polish and the spray cleaners will leave your windows clean and crystal clear.

Engine cleaner
One part of your car that shouldn't be neglected when it come to cleaning – even though it won't need cleaning as often as the rest of your car, and you won't see much of it – is the engine bay.

You don't generally need many cleaners for this part of your car, as once it has been washed off it can be left to dry, then finished off with some of the products that you'll be using on other parts of your car (explained in a later chapter). For now, you'll just need to add an engine degreaser and combined cleaner to your shopping list.

In this particular instance, I recommend that you use Autoglym Engine & Machine Cleaner: it does the whole job in one go, and you won't need other products. It's a really powerful, but non-corrosive cleaner for your engine, which comes in a handy trigger-spray bottle, and works as a detergent and a degreaser.

It's also safe to use this product on metal, paintwork, rubber, and plastic, as it contains no nasty solvents. Water-based and biodegradable, it will clean the whole engine and engine bay quickly – just spray it on to your engine and around the engine bay, agitate stubborn grime or grease with a stiff brush, then simply wash off and leave to dry.

Polishes and waxes
Finally, to finish off the exterior of your car you'll need a good quality polish and one of the many sealants or waxes that are now available. These are optional, but using one will give your car's paintwork some extra protection from everyday contaminates and dirt, and will keep your paintwork looking nice and glossy for much longer.

Sealants are quite different from polishes, as they don't contain any cleaning or polishing agents, and are made from tough resins and, usually, a mix of waxes.

Waxes are another form of sealant which protect your paintwork from contamination. They'll also enhance the existing finish, so you should make sure your paintwork is clean and in good condition (not faded, for instance) before applying a wax finish – otherwise you'll simply be sealing in any poor finish you already have.

A polish will lightly clean any remaining dirt from the surface of your car, leaving a nice shine. There are lots of polishes on the market, some of which will fill minor imperfections and scratches. Others will renovate faded or oxidised paintwork, restoring its original lustre. Once polished, you can apply the sealant, a wax, or even both, which will give you a really rich, deep, long-lasting, beautiful shine that is both tough and durable.

Interior cleaning
So, that's what you'll need for the exterior of your car. There are just a few more items to help with cleaning the interior, and then we can move on to tools. Fewer products are needed for the interior, one of which I've already mentioned: vinyl cleaner. This is good for general cleaning of interior surfaces, and along with that you'll need a silicone-free spray to give your surfaces a nice sheen. I suggest the silicone-free type as it tends to be less messy in use, and won't become tacky and attract dust.

I have also already mentioned glass polish for use on your windows and interior mirrors, so that just leaves an interior shampoo, for cleaning your carpets, upholstery, and for removing stains, general dirt, and marks from spillages or pets.

For leather interiors, you'll need a leather cleaner, along with a leather cream or balm, and to complete the collection, an odour eliminator and air fresheners.

There are generally two types of shampoo: one comes in aerosol form, that when sprayed onto your seats and carpets turns into a foam; the other is a spray-on liquid, and this is the one I have chosen for the purposes of this book.

Leather cleaners come in a trigger-spray bottle, usually sprayed directly onto your leather, and removed with a soft cloth. After cleaning, you'll need to apply the leather balm. This contains natural oils and soaps to nourish, moisturise, and provide protection for your car's leather. Regular applications will help preserve the natural appearance and characteristics of your leather, and, as an added benefit, will make cleaning easier, as dirt will not adhere to, or penetrate, the surface of the leather so easily.

Odour eliminators come as a spray, and air fresheners come in many forms and fragrances: card types that hang from a rear-view mirror, control stalk, or switch; stick-on types, in many different shapes and designs, that can be stuck to windows or fascias; and granular ones for filling an ash tray or similar container.

There is another form of air freshener: an aerosol type that, for obvious reasons, doesn't last as long, but may be able to be sprayed directly onto seats and carpets (check the directions on the can first), which tend to hold odours.

Tools & cleaning aids

To start with, you'll need a decent size bucket – a builder's bucket is ideal and they're pretty tough, too. You'll also need a couple of good sized sponges or a wash mitt. As the name suggests, wash mitts are worn on your hand like a mitten, they have lots of short 'tentacles' or 'noodles' on them, and are made from microfibre, which is very soft and absorbent.

You'll find a wheel brush invaluable for removing stubborn baked-on brake dust, and also for use on the engine, on grease and grime that sometimes needs a bit of persuasion to shift. They're made from tough materials that will stand up to vigorous use and should last you a good few years. Buy the type that has a conical bristle head – they're great for getting into hard to reach places.

Drying
After washing your car, you'll need to dry it to prevent streaks and run marks, and also to leave a good finish ready for polishing. For this, you'll need either a genuine chamois leather, a synthetic chamois, or a microfibre drying towel.

Chamois leathers do a great job of drying your car, but are expensive and can be hard work to use. You'll also have to keep it damp at all times when stored: if it dries out, it becomes hard and is no longer usable. Some synthetic chamois are very good: the Autoglym Aqua-dry and the Vileda Flunky being two such examples (both can be found online).

Finally, microfibre drying towels are also very good, and are made by many different companies. Being highly absorbent, they dry your car quite quickly, once you get used to using them. I mainly use a synthetic chamois, as it's cost effective and long lasting, but I do sometimes use microfibre drying towels if time is short, as they do dry your car a little quicker. A squeegee or flexible water blade is another tool which can save you some work and cut drying time quite considerably.

Miscellaneous tools

Well, that's the tools for washing and drying your car sorted out, now for the rest of the tools:

A few good size cloths for applying polishes – one for glass and one for the bodywork, and the rest for use with the other cleaners. I recommend using 100% cotton cloths, as cloths containing man-made fibres can leave fine scratches on your car's paintwork. Rolls of stockinette are very useful: you can cut off a piece just the right size for the job and, as it's reasonably priced, when it gets worn out or dirty you can just dispose of it and cut off some more.

Quick tip: before using your freshly cut stockinette, give it a good shake, as it does tend to shed a few fibres whilst in use (if you've just vacuumed your car, you don't want bits of cloth all over the seats and carpets).

For removing polish and buffing-up your paintwork to a brilliant shine, I highly recommend using microfibre cloths. They leave your car with a beautiful glass-like finish and are easy to use.

If you're a dog owner, a pet hair removal brush will come in very handy for your interior. Made from rubber, with soft latex nodules that 'grab' the pet hair, it brushes hair into bunches for easy removal by hand or with the vacuum cleaner.

A 2in paintbrush is a useful tool for getting into places like air vents to remove dust.

Finally, a blade holder and some blades are another very handy addition

for when you need to remove stickers from your windows, or stubborn dead flies from your windscreen/windshield when all else fails!

Hoses and washers

Last, but by no means least, you'll need a hose pipe, or better still, a pressure washer for rinsing off your car once it's been washed. We'll assume that you already have a hose, but if not, then just an ordinary garden hose with an adjustable spray/jet nozzle will do.

A pressure washer will make cleaning your car's wheels, wheelarches and door shuts easier, and will speed up the rinsing off process. They are available from many car care and DIY/ garden centres for very reasonable prices. **Caution!** The high pressure jet could damage paintwork, door seals and electrical items if you get too close.

We all have vacuum cleaners, but if you have an upright type, then you'll need the extension hose for reaching into your car. Whichever type you own, you'll need to use a crevice tool for getting into awkward places, like under and between the seats.

If you decide to purchase a vacuum cleaner specifically for cleaning your car, I highly recommend either a 'Henry' or a 'George' (both manufactured by Numatic). Henry is a powerful little vacuum cleaner that's very reliable and perfect for cleaning cars. His 'bigger brother,' George, has the added benefit of a shampoo function, and is a model that I have used for nearly ten years with very few problems and great results.

Finally, on the following page you'll find the list that I promised you at the beginning of this chapter. Once you've gathered all these items together, we'll be ready to start: enjoy your shopping!

CLEANING PRODUCTS LIST

- ❏ Bodywork shampoo/conditioner.
- ❏ Tar remover.
- ❏ Wheel cleaner – non-acid-based.
- ❏ Wheel cleaner – acid-based.
- ❏ Tyre dressing/renovator, spray-on or foam.
- ❏ Insect/bug remover.
- ❏ Vinyl/rubber care (a gel type that you spray or squeeze onto a cloth is best).
- ❏ Cabriolet owners will need a hood cleaner plus protector/reproofer which comes as a kit.
- ❏ Glass polish, wax and silicone free and a glass cleaner spray.
- ❏ Resin polish.
- ❏ Interior shampoo (for carpets, upholstery etc)
- ❏ Leather cleaner.
- ❏ Leather care balm.
- ❏ Odour eliminator.
- ❏ Air freshener.

Optional products

- ❏ Clay bar kit. (See How and why to use a clay bar, on page 43)
- ❏ Paint sealant, Autoglym extra gloss protection, or equivalent.
- ❏ High definition wax or equivalent.
- ❏ Silicone-free spray for fascia and other interior surfaces.

TOOLS LIST

- ❏ Bucket (I use a builder's bucket).
- ❏ Two large sponges or a microfibre wash mitt.
- ❏ Wheel brush (conical bristle shape).
- ❏ Chamois leather (synthetic/genuine) or microfibre drying towel.
- ❏ Microfibre cloths for removing polish.
- ❏ Blade holder and blades.
- ❏ 2in/5cm paint brush (for cleaning vents etc).
- ❏ A hose pipe.
- ❏ Vacuum cleaner. I would highly recommend a Henry, but if you're going to use your existing vacuum, make sure you have a crevice tool.

Optional tools

- ❏ Squeegee or water blade.
- ❏ Roll of stockinette.
- ❏ Pet hair removal brush.
- ❏ Pressure washer.
- ❏ George wet & dry vacuum cleaner.

two

Preparing your car for washing

How, where, and when to clean

Now that you have everything you need, we can get started – but first, there are a few things that we have to consider. The first one is; how often should we clean our cars? Of course, the answer depends very much on how often your car is used, and what it's used for. If, for instance, you only use your car for daily travel to and from work, then most of the time it will be either parked in a car park or parking lot, on the roadside, or – best of all – parked in a garage or covered lot.

If this sounds like your car, then a wash-off once every two weeks will probably be sufficient, followed up with a full clean inside and out every four to six weeks. However, if your car is used for work, shopping, transporting the kids to and from school, plus various other activities over the weekend, such as an occasional trip to the recycling centre or refuse tip, then you'll need to clean your car much more frequently to keep it in tip-top condition. As a guide, I usually recommend a good wash-off and vacuum once a week, followed by a regular monthly clean, which should include wheels and wheelarches, to help prevent the build-up of brake dust that becomes baked-on and difficult to remove with normal cleaning.

I am regularly asked, "How often should I polish my car?" The simple answer to that is, as with washing, it depends on how often you use your car, where it's usually parked, and the weather conditions it's been subjected to. As a general rule-of-thumb, I polish metallic paintwork every eight weeks, and flat paint or Clear Coat finishes every six to eight weeks.

Where to clean
We should now consider where we will be cleaning our car. If you have a driveway, that's probably the

Fig 1. The first step in a thorough clean is to remove loose dirt.

straightforward answer to where. However, if you don't have a driveway, your next best alternative will usually be the roadside outside your house. If this happens to be the case, you need to consider the safety issues.

Whenever I have to clean a car on the roadside, I always wear a 'High visibility' vest over my clothes. These are inexpensive and are available from many outlets, such as your local DIY store. It may sound a little extreme, but it could potentially save you from serious injury, or even save your life. Of course, you should use your own judgement here:

you'll know how busy your road gets.

One quick word on driveways: if you have a gravel driveway, then you'll need to take extra care if you're going to be using a pressure washer. I have seen many cars damaged by flying gravel caused by someone inadvertently holding the lance of a pressure washer a little too low.

When to clean
The first thing to consider here, is the weather. You should avoid – if at all possible – cleaning your car in full sun, especially if it's a dark colour. The

Fig 2. Flush-out the wheelarches to remove mud and other contaminants.

Fig 3. Insect remains.

Fig 4. Spray insect remains to soften.

reason for this is that once you have washed off your car, it will dry very quickly, leaving nasty runs and streaks. These not only look unsightly, but also make polishing harder. Plus, if you're only giving your car a weekly wash-off, you'll end up having to polish it just to remove the streaks.

The best time to clean your car is usually early morning or late afternoon, and early evening during the summer, as this is when the sun is not so

Fig 5. Wipe over to remove softened remains.

fierce. If cleaning in bright sunlight is unavoidable, then try to find some partial shade – a tree perhaps, or if possible park your car within the shade of your house or other building. Start washing it on the shaded side first, and dry it starting from the side exposed to the sun.

Once the summer is over, we're faced with the challenge of finding a day to clean the car that isn't damp or, worse still, raining. If you own or have access to a garage big enough to house your car, with room enough for you to work around it, then once washed off, you can move into the garage for the rest of the cleaning process. Don't forget, though, that artificial light is never as good as natural light, and you'll want to give your handywork a good once over outside, in natural light, after the weather has improved. You can then put right anything that you've missed, or buff up any smears on paintwork or glass.

Preparing the car for washing

So, now we know where, when, and how often we should clean our car, lets

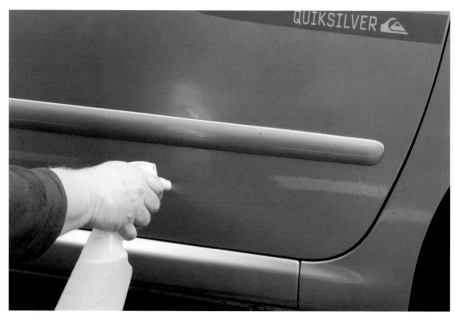

Fig 6. Spray on tar remover and leave to dissolve the tar spots.

get started. If your car is heavily soiled, it's a good idea to first run the hose/ pressure washer over the bodywork to remove any loose material such as, mud, grit, and sand (Fig 1). If left on the car when you start to wash it, these particles will be picked up by your sponge or wash mitt and leave minute scratches in the surface of the paintwork. For this reason, if you happen to drop your sponge or wash mitt whilst washing your car, ensure you rinse it in clean water until there are no particles of dirt or grit clinging to it, before continuing to use it – even better, use another sponge.

Wheelarches
It's a great idea at this point to give the wheelarches a good spray with the hose/ pressure washer to remove any mud and contaminates picked up from the roads whilst driving (Fig 2). Once any excess dirt has been removed, we can then continue with the preparation for

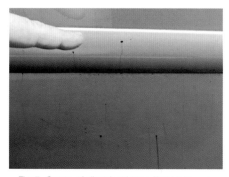

Fig 7. Spots of dissolved tar will start to run.

washing-off. If there are insect remains on the front of your car (Fig 3), you'll now need to spray the affected area with insect remover (Fig 4). Once you've given a liberal coating, leave for around 30 seconds to soften, then wipe off with a cloth (Fig 5). If there are any remains left on the car, simply give the area another spray immediately before washing.

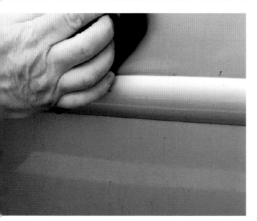

Fig 8. Wipe over the treated area to remove dissolved tar spots.

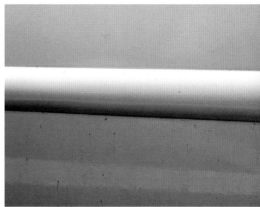

Fig 9. Here, tar spots above trim have been removed.

Lower bodywork

The next step is to check the lower sections of your car for spots of tar. If you find any, squirt some tar remover directly onto the area (Fig 6), wait for a few seconds, and the tar spots should begin to run (Fig 7). You'll now be able to rub the spots with a soft cloth (Fig 8) to remove the tar. As with insect remains, if any tar spots remain, give it another light squirt of tar remover just before washing-off to remove these last traces (Fig 9).

Fig 10. Dirty filler cap flap and recess.

Fig 11. Spray with tar remover to dissolve the dirt.

Fig 12. A quick wash-off with clean water completes the job.

Fuel filler cap

Check around the recess and flap of the fuel filler cap. This area can become very dirty with fuel contamination, which becomes sticky and attracts particles of grit and dust, etc, (Fig 10).

Give the area a spray with the tar remover (Fig 11), leave for a few seconds, then wash-off the dirt with a hose or pressure washer (Fig 12). Again, any remaining stubborn dirt should be sprayed again just before washing-off (Fig 13).

Fig 13. The finished area – nice and clean.

Fig 14. Spray the door shuts with tar remover.

Fig 15. After spraying, rinse at high pressure.

Fig 16. Do the same with the other doors.

Door shuts

Next, clean the door shuts and hinges. Open the doors one at a time and spray around the shuts and hinges with tar remover or engine cleaner (Fig 14). This will dissolve grease and grime making it easy to remove. Treat each door the same way, including the boot/trunk lid or rear hatch. After a few minutes you can rinse with your hose or pressure washer (Fig 15). High pressure is good

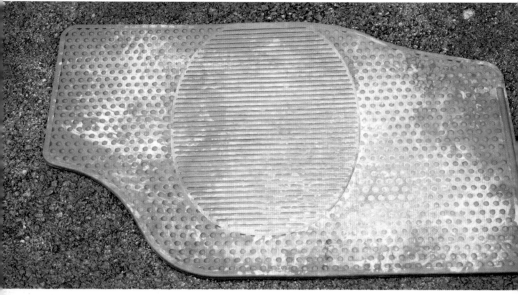

Fig 17. In need of a clean.

Fig 18. A good sponge-off with soapy water.

Fig 19. A high pressure rinse will finish the job.

here, so if you're using a hose, adjusting the nozzle to get a jet is a good idea, as this removes the dissolved dirt more thoroughly (Fig 16).

Rubber mats
Whilst you have the hose/pressure washer to hand, give the car's rubber mats a clean, if it has them. First, wash them with soapy water (Fig 17 & 18), then spray-off with lots of clean water from the hose or washer (Fig 19).

Wheels
The final step in preparing your car for washing-off is to ensure the wheels are nice and clean. Make sure that the wheels are cool before you start,

Fig 20. Spray wheels with plenty of cleaner.

Fig 21. Agitate with a stiff wheel brush.

Fig 22. Pay attention to the wheel nuts and recesses.

otherwise you'll find them difficult to clean as the wheel cleaner will simply evaporate if sprayed onto hot wheel rims.

Spray the wheels with plenty of wheel cleaner (Fig 20), leave for a few seconds, then agitate with the wheel brush to loosen any stubborn dirt and brake dust (Fig 21). Ensure you get into all the corners and pay particular attention to the wheel nuts and their recesses (Fig 22). Now you can simply rinse off using the hose or washer. As with the door shuts, using a good jet of water will give the wheels a proper rinse, taking the dirt and brake dust with it (Fig 23).

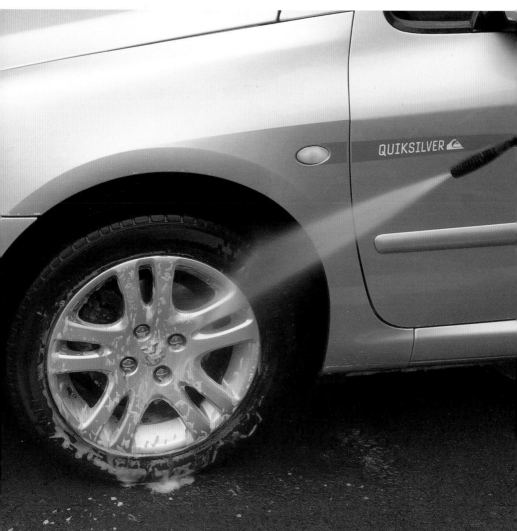

Fig 23. Finally, a good rinse off with a high pressure hose.

three

Cleaning a soft top/ convertible hood

Owning a convertible requires an extra task when cleaning your car. However, it's a very simple one, and it won't take very long to achieve great results. That task is, of course, keeping your car's hood clean.

When to clean

I recommend cleaning your hood twice a year. The first clean should take place in the early part of the year, around March or April, when the weather has started to warm up a little. This means your hood will not only dry quicker, but will look nice and clean and fresh after the rigours of the winter weather, ready for the summer.

The second clean should be around September or October, after summer but before the winter weather really sets in. In the UK, we still have some mild (even warm) days at this time of year, which are ideal to clean, refresh, and protect your hood in readiness for the cold and wet months to come.

There are many hood cleaners and protectors on the market, so the best idea is to buy a hood cleaning kit. This will give you everything you need to remove the dirt and grime from your car's hood, and then reproof it to protect it against dirt, traffic film, and water absorption.

How to clean

I suggest that you carry out this task before you give your car the final wash-off. Then, overspray from the hood cleaning products will be removed when you wash the car.

For this chapter I will be using the Autoglym Hood Cleaning Kit (Fig 24), but if you're using another brand check the supplied instructions before commencing.

Start by giving the hood a good brush off with a stiff brush to remove any loose material from its surface. Or, if you prefer, you could use your vacuum cleaner (Fig 25), but take care not to

Fig 24. Autoglym's hood cleaning kit.

Fig 25. Remove loose dirt with a brush or vacuum.

use too much pressure, or you could leave marks on the hood.

After brushing or vacuuming, take your hose or pressure washer and wet the hood: **don't use high pressure** – this can leave marks on the fabric. If using a pressure washer, you may need to stand back a few feet from the car (Fig 26).

Once you have wet the hood you can start to apply the cleaner (Fig 27). Give the hood a good even coating of

Fig 26. Wet the hood before applying the cleaner.

Fig 27. Spray the hood evenly with the cleaner.

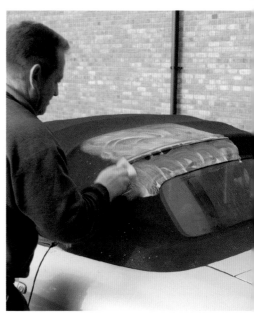

Fig 28. Agitate the cleaner with the sponge provided.

cleaner, but don't saturate it. Once half of the hood is covered with cleaner, use the sponge that comes with the cleaning kit (or a scrubbing brush, used lightly) to gently agitate the cleaner. This will create a light foam (Fig 28).

Now move to the other side of your car and repeat; spray on the cleaner and gently agitate (Fig 29). You may need to apply a little more pressure in

Fig 29. Make sure you get into any tight seams.

Fig 30. Dirt and green algae can collect in seams.

Fig 31. Rinse the hood well until the water runs clear.

some areas, such as seams, as dirt and algae accumulate here (Fig 30).

Once you've thoroughly cleaned the whole hood, you can take your hose or pressure washer and gently rinse off the cleaner (Fig 31), until the water that is running off the hood is clear.

Reproofing

Now you need to reproof the hood. Take the reproofer and spray it onto the hood (Fig 32). Give it a generous coat, but, again, you don't need to saturate the fabric. It's best to reproof whilst the hood is still damp, as the proofing will be absorbed into the fabric much quicker.

That's it! You now have a nice clean and refreshed hood that's once again protected against dirt, traffic film, and water absorption.

Note: If you own a car that has a vinyl or plastic hood, you can use Autoglym Interior Shampoo to clean it, followed by a light coat of Autoglym Bumper Care vinyl gel to protect it.

Fig 32. Spray on the reproofer to protect the hood.

four
How to clean your car's engine safely

When it comes to cleaning your car's engine there are a few precautions you need to take before you start. First, don't attempt to clean your car's engine if it's still hot from use. A hot engine can cause a serious burn if you happen to touch the wrong part.

Also, if you spray engine cleaner onto a hot engine, it will simply evaporate before it has a chance to do its job. **Note:** some engine cleaners suggest that you use them on a slightly *warm* engine, which can help to soften and loosen dirt and grime.

Fig 33. Note the protection over the electrics.

Fig 34. Engine & Machine Cleaner, plus a stiff brush.

Protect the electrics

Once the engine is cool, the first thing you must do before applying the cleaner is to protect electrical connections and items such as the alarm system. This can be done using cling film/Saran wrap and/or a food/freezer bag and rubber band to secure it (Fig 33).

Caution! If you are not absolutely confident you can protect the electrics, leave engine cleaning to a professional.

Apply the cleaner

Once these parts have been covered, you can spray on the engine cleaner (Fig 34), making sure you cover the whole engine and get into all the corners and crevices of the engine bay (Fig 35). Leave the cleaner to soak for a minute or two, to soften the grease and grime (Fig 36), then take your wheel brush (or other stiff brush) and agitate the cleaner (Fig 37), again making sure you get into all the corners and crevices that you sprayed cleaner into.

You may need to brush some

Fig 35. Ensure you get cleaner into all the corners.

Fig 36. Give a good covering of cleaner and leave to soak.

Fig 37. Agitate stubborn dirt.

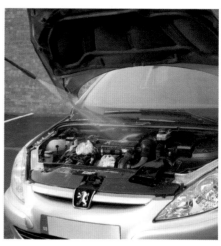

Fig 38. Rinse well.

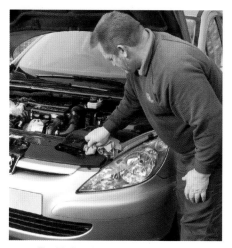

Fig 39. Dry the wettest parts with a chamois.

Fig 40. Spray with vinyl care, then wipe away the excess.

areas with a little more effort to remove stubborn or ground-in dirt and grime, and I sometimes use an old toothbrush for getting into some of the smaller spaces between cables or pipes.

Rinsing and finishing

Now you can simply rinse off the engine with your hose or pressure washer (Fig 38). Stand back a few feet if your washer doesn't adjust to low pressure. Once rinsed off, use your chamois to dry the wettest parts (Fig 39) and around the engine bay, then leave the parts that you cannot reach to air dry.

To give the engine a good finish, spray some Vinyl & Rubber Care over it (Fig 40) and wipe over with a soft cloth to remove the excess. This leaves a nice sheen on components such as the air filter cover and fuse box.

Finally, don't forget to remove the cling film/Saran wrap or food/freezer bags that you used to protect the electrical connections! (Fig 41).

Fig 41. Gleaming! Don't forget to remove the protection from electrical items.

five

Washing & drying your car

In this chapter I'll be showing you how to wash and dry your car effectively, giving you the best results in preparation for polishing. By now you'll have cleaned your car's convertible hood (if it has one), and removed contaminates such as insect remains and road tar from the bodywork. The wheels will have been cleaned and, if needed, you'll have followed the instructions in chapter 4 and cleaned your engine too. So, we can now move on and wash the rest of the car ... let's get started.

Washing

Add some car shampoo/conditioner to your bucket in accordance with the manufacturers guidelines. Fill the bucket with cold or warm water (whichever you prefer), then add a sponge or a wash mitt to the water. We'll begin by washing the roof (Fig 42). Use plenty of water and long sweeping strokes of the sponge/

Fig 42. Start by washing the roof.

Fig 43. Work around and down the car.

Fig 44. Wash the lower sections of the car last.

wash mitt. When you've cleaned half the roof, work your way down the side of the car (Fig 43) and wash the windows. Then move around to the back and across the rear window. You can now wash the other half of the roof, windows, and lastly the windscreen/windshield.

You may find it easier to wash the windsceen/windshield if you first 'park' the wipers in the up position – this will allow easier access to the scuttle and around the base of the wipers. If this isn't possible with your car, gently lift each wiper blade as you wash, then lower them slowly back to the screen.

Now that the top half of the car has been washed, you can start to work your way around the rest of the car, leaving the bottom of the panels and the wheels until last (Fig 44).

Bird droppings
If you notice patches of bird droppings when washing, never simply wash over them with your sponge/wash mitt. Bird droppings contain grit and other hard contaminants, and washing over them will almost certainly damage the paintwork. First use a separate sponge, that has been soaked in soapy water, to sit on the patch of bird droppings and soften it for a few minutes (Fig 46). It will then be safe to *gently* remove the droppings using plenty of soapy water. If the droppings are on the side of the car, you may find it easier to place a wet cloth on them. Failing this, you'll have to hold the sponge or cloth on the area for a minute or two, until the droppings are softened enough to remove safely.

One final tip on bird droppings: don't, if at all possible, leave them on your car for any length of time. If you do, it's highly likely that they will permanently damage the paintwork, leaving a patch of flat or dull paint. Always try to remove droppings as soon as you can.

Fig 45. Hardened bird droppings.

Fig 46. Soak with a wet sponge to soften.

Fig 47. Don't miss the recesses.

Continue washing with the bonnet/ hood, the front wing/fender, and then move on to the front door, then the rear door (if its a four-door car), and finally the rear quarter. Wash off the boot/trunk lid or hatchback next, making sure you get into the recess of the number/licence plate (Fig 47), and any other features (such as manufacturer's badges and radio aerial/antenna). Then continue along the other side of the car.

Whilst washing your car, you should rinse the sponge/wash mitt regularly to remove particles of dirt that may cling to it. You should also avoid dipping your sponge/wash mitt right to the bottom of the bucket, as this is where all the particles of dirt and grime will settle. If you pick up any of this dirt, not only will you deposit it back on your nice clean car, but it could damage the

paintwork. For the same reason, don't be tempted to throw water remaining in your bucket over the car; just tip it down the drain.

Rinsing

We must now rinse the car to remove the soap suds and any remaining dirt particles. If you're using a pressure washer, then you should adjust it to low pressure, as we want lots of water to flush away the soapy water. If you can't lower the pressure on your washer, don't worry – simply stand back from the car when rinsing-off (Figs 48, 49 and 50).

Rinsing should be done in the same order as washing: start with the roof, flushing the car with lots of water to remove all the soap and remaining dirt.

Fig 48. Begin rinsing from the roof.

Fig 49. Work down the sides.

Fig 50. Pressure wash the sills.

When you get to the wheelarches you can use high pressure again, giving them a good rinse out, and ensuring that all the dirt has been flushed away. Finally, give the wheels a good rinse, too.

Drying

Once we have rinsed the car, we need to dry it thoroughly in readiness for polishing. If you're going to use a water blade (squeegee), make sure it's spotlessly clean before bringing it into contact with your car's paintwork.

I usually start by drying the windows (Fig 51), then dry one side (that way I don't get wet when I reach across the roof). If using a water blade, run it down the windows from top to bottom, then along the doors, wings/fenders, and rear quarter. This will remove most of the water (Fig 52), letting you finish off with either a microfibre drying towel or a chamois (after which a quick wring-

Fig 51. Dry thoroughly with a chamois or towel.

41

Fig 52. Water blades can save a lot of time.

out and shake will get rid of any dirt particles).

Once you've dried one side of the car, you can move on to the roof. This is where a water blade can really help: it will quickly clear water from the roof, with a wipe over with a chamois finishing the job. if you prefer to use a chamois or drying towel without a water blade, that's fine; you'll just need to wring it out more frequently.

Now for the windscreen/windshield. Gently lift the wipers, dry the screen and the wiper blades, then lower them slowly back to the screen. Run the water blade down the bonnet/hood to remove the majority of the water, then finish with the chamois. Repeat on the other side of the car, roof, and then the rear window, finally drying the boot/trunk lid or hatchback. Use a separate chamois to dry the wheels, and you're almost finished.

All that's left now is to dry the door shuts and doors. Open the doors and boot/trunk lid or hatchback, and wipe around them with your chamois or drying towel (Fig 53). That's it: you're almost ready to polish your car. Have a final walk around your car, to make sure you haven't missed anything (Fig 54) and, if you're happy, you can now get started on the polishing.

Fig 53. Don't forget to dry the door shuts.

Fig 54. Clean and dry.

six

How & why to use a clay bar

How clean is your car?

This may seem like a strange question, given the fact that we've just taken a step-by-step look at traffic film removal, wheel cleaning, and washing and drying your car. But even all these processes combined cannot remove all of the contaminates that your car will pick up during everyday use.

Most of the contamination on your car's paintwork is actually microscopic metallic particles. Some of these particles are produced by railway/railroad trains when braking, and from the friction of their wheels on the tracks. These microscopic metal particles, known as 'rail dust,' are very hot, and once they become airborne they can embed themselves into the surface of your car's paintwork.

Although this is quite a severe form of contamination, it's actually very commonplace – especially if you happen to live near, or regularly travel close to, a railway/railroad station or tracks.

Even a new car straight from a dealership could have this type of contamination, as manufacturers often store new vehicles (in huge numbers) outside and unprotected from the elements, and many of these storage areas are close to railways/railroads. These, in turn, are often close to industrial sites, which are yet another source of contamination. Tree sap, brake dust, and general industrial pollutants are also common contaminates that bond to your car's paintwork.

It can be quite hard to see these tiny metal particles on dark-coloured cars, but you'll definitely be able to feel them. When you run your hand over the paintwork, it will feel rough – in some cases it can feel like running your hand across sandpaper! On lighter colours, these particles can often be seen, as

Fig 55. A good quality clay bar kit.

they turn brown as they oxidise and turn to rust.

This may all sound rather worrying, but there's a solution that means we can have our car's paintwork looking and feeling silky smooth again. All your car needs is a 'clay bar' treatment. Clay bars very effectively and safely remove these contaminants. It won't cut into your paintwork like a cutting polish, but works by 'grabbing' and 'pulling' contaminants off of the surface.

The clay bar kit I will be using (Fig 55), contains a spray-on lubricant, a clay bar, and a microfibre cloth. It's very important that you use a lubricant, otherwise you could scratch the surface of the paint. For the same reason, it's also very important that you only carry out this procedure after thoroughly washing and drying your car.

Using a clay bar

To use a clay bar, first take it out of the pack (Fig 56) and start to 'knead' it, softening it ready for use. If it's a cold day, you can dip the clay bar in warm water to help soften it. Once softened, you'll need to pull off a small piece of the clay – just enough so that when

Fig 56. Remove a small piece of clay and knead.

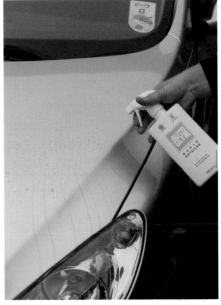

Fig 57. Spray the panel to be clayed with plenty of lubricant.

flattened, it's just covered by three of your fingers.

You're now ready to start. The best place to do this is the roof or bonnet/hood, then work your way around and down the car. Work in a small area at a time: for instance, the roof would be divided into four sections, as would the bonnet/hood, etc.

Spray plenty of the lubricant onto the panel (Fig 57), and some onto your piece of clay (Fig 58). Rub the clay in a back-and-forth motion across the panel (Fig 59), spraying more lubricant if needed. Keep rubbing until the paintwork feels silky smooth, then wipe over the panel with the microfibre cloth to remove the lubricant (Fig 60).

Now, simply fold and knead your piece of clay to create a nice clean side, and start again on another section of the panel. Don't forget: use **plenty** of lubricant.

Fig 58. Spray the clay with lubricant, too.

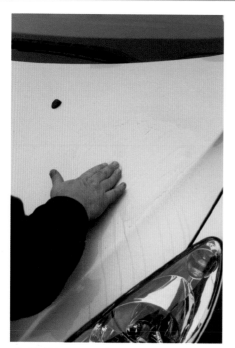

Fig 59. Work the clay bar using back-and-forth strokes.

Fig 60. Remove lubricant with a microfibre cloth.

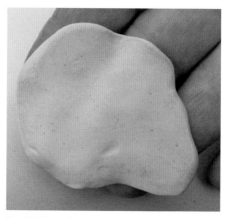

Fig 61. Use a fresh piece of clean clay when the piece you're using becomes dirty.

Once the clay has become too dirty to enable you to create a clean side, you should discard it and pull off a new piece from bar (Fig 61). If after completing a panel your piece of clay isn't too dirty, you could use it to remove baked-on brake dust from your alloy wheels before discarding it. You can also use a clay bar on glass, and it can be used to great effect to remove embedded dead flies and other insects.

Once the clay bar process is complete, your paint should feel silky-smooth and be ready for polishing. A clay bar treatment twice a year is more than adequate for most cars, although you may like to repeat this procedure more often if, for instance, your car isn't garaged, or you live or work in an area where there are many industrial buildings – or you live close to a railway!

seven
Polishing bodywork & glass

Polishing is probably the one job that has the biggest impact on the overall look of a finished car. It's also one of the most satisfying and pleasurable elements of cleaning a car, too. Personally, I find polishing a car very therapeutic, and as long as the car's bodywork has been prepared as described in the preceding chapters, and you use a good quality polish, then this very important process shouldn't be hard work.

Polishing your car the right way, with a good quality polish (Fig 62), will give your car's bodywork a rich, deep, long-lasting and durable shine. This not only makes your car a pleasure to drive, but it also helps to preserve its resale value.

Applying polish

To apply the polish, first take a soft, clean and dry cloth (you should only

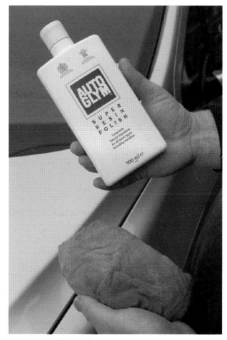

Fig 62. A good quality resin polish.

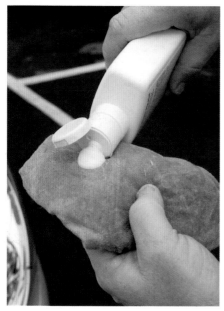

Fig 63. Squeeze the polish onto a cotton cloth.

use a 100% cotton cloth), and squeeze a small amount of polish onto it (Fig 63). You don't need a large amount; about the size of a 5p coin/dime, as it will spread quite a long way. If you use too much, not only will you be wasting polish, but it will take longer to dry and be harder to remove.

Start with the roof or the bonnet/hood, and apply the polish with an overlapping circular motion. Before it dries, even-out the polish with long straight sweeping strokes, along the length of the car (Fig 64). Now work your way around the car until all the panels are evenly covered with polish. As you work around the car, refold your polishing cloth every so often, to prevent reapplying dirt particles that may have been picked up back onto your paintwork. If the weather is looking changeable, it may be a good idea to polish only a couple of panels at a time;

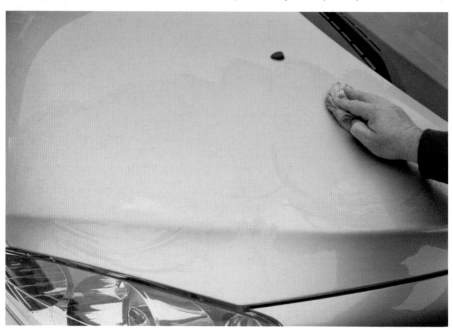

Fig 64. Apply the polish using a circular motion.

Fig 65. Remove polish in the same manner as it was applied.

Fig 66. Drain water traps with a chamois.

that way, if it does start to rain, you'll have less polish to wash off before starting again.

Removing polish

Once the polish is dry you can start to remove it with a clean microfibre cloth (Fig 65). Follow the same sequence as you did when you applied the polish. You may encounter a few water traps whilst polishing your car, typical areas being door mirrors, window seals, and fuel filler flaps. These can be very annoying, however, if it's only a *small* amount of water, you can just carry on and ignore it (whether you're applying polish or removing it).

However, if quite a large amount of water is leaking over the polished area, you'll need to soak it up before continuing, otherwise it will cause smearing and spoil the finish. Take a chamois or drying towel, and hold it on the offending water trap (Fig 66): this should soak up the remaining water – or if you own a wet and dry vacuum, such as a Vax or a George, you can use it to suck out the remaining water. Once done, you can continue with the polishing.

Take care when applying the polish not to get it on plastic or vinyl trim and window rubbers, as it will turn white and look untidy, spoiling the finish. If you do happen to get polish on any of these parts, you can remove it with vinyl care spray or gel applied with a cloth. If the trim is textured, you may need to agitate it a little (an old toothbrush is ideal for this purpose).

Polishing glass

Now that the bodywork polishing is finished, we can move on to the glass. Start with the interior of the windows, applying a small amount of glass polish (again, about the size of a 5p coin/dime, or less) to a soft, dry, clean cotton cloth (Fig 67). Then, as with the bodywork, apply the glass polish with an overlapping circular motion (Fig 68), until you reach the edges of the window. Finish with straight lines, and avoid getting polish on the interior trim as, again, it may cause marks (as with the exterior polish, these can be removed using the same method).

Once you've applied polish to all of the windows' interior surfaces, you

Fig 67. Squeeze glass polish onto a cotton cloth.

Fig 69. Don't forget the interior mirrors.

Fig 68. Apply polish to the inside of the glass first.

can polish the interior mirrors (Fig 69), and after allowing a few minutes for the polish to dry thoroughly, you can remove it.

Once you've finished the interior, you can continue with the exterior glass (Fig 70). Apply the polish in the same manner as with the interior, including the door mirrors (Fig 71), and once dry, buff-off with a microfibre cloth (Figs 72 & 73), and that's it.

Fig 72. Buff-up the exterior glass.

Fig 70. Now for the outside of the glass.

Fig 71. Give the door mirrors a polish, too.

Fig 73. Remove the polish from the door mirrors.

eight
Vacuming the interior of your car

Vacuuming the interior of your car is a very important part of the cleaning process. Apart from the obvious benefit of driving a nice clean and tidy car, regular vacuuming helps to preserve the life of your car's carpets.

When getting into a car and stepping onto the carpets, dirt and grit on the carpet and on your shoes is ground further into the fibres, and with regular use the carpets eventually wear thin and develop holes. With regular cleaning, this process is minimised.

The best tool/accessory I have found for vacuuming a car is the 'crevice' tool (Fig 74), as it gets into all the awkward-to-reach and small spaces with relative ease.

I usually start at the driver's seat

Fig 74. The crevice tool – the best tool for the job.

Fig 75. I start at the driver's seat.

(Fig 75), then move on to the driver's footwell, working my way around the car anti-clockwise, before finishing with the front passenger seat and footwell – but work around your car whichever way you prefer.

Start with the headrest (Fig 76), then the back rest, and finally the seat pad. If you have 'sculpted' seats, or stitching within the seat design, you'll need to place your hand on the seat close to the sculpted area and press down: this will open up the crease created by the sculpting, and you'll be better able to vacuum up accumulated dirt and debris (Fig 77).

Next, you'll need to adjust the seat, pushing it back as far as it will go towards the rear of the car. This will give better access to the area beneath the seat. Once you've removed any debris from this area, continue vacuuming, not forgetting the area at the side of the seat (Fig 78). Move into the footwell area (Fig 79) to complete this section, and

Fig 76. Vacuum the headrest first.

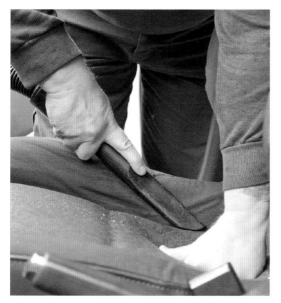

Fig 78. Common dirt traps.

Fig 77. Push down on sculpted seats to better access dirt and debris.

Fig 79. Clean down by the sides of the seats.

Fig 80. Vacuum under the seats, too.

Fig 81. Clean behind the backrests of the seats.

Fig 82. The boot/trunk will also need a good vacuuming.

then move on to the rear seat behind the seat you've just completed.

Again, start with the headrest, and work down the seat and across the seat pad. If your car is a hatchback or estate/station wagon, you'll have folding seats: you should lift the seat pad and vacuum the area underneath (Fig 80). When you've completed this, release the back rest and pull it forward, giving you access to the space behind (Fig 81). Replace the seat to its original position once finished.

Next, the boot/trunk area. This area, by default, tends to get dirtier than the rest of the car, so will probably need a bit more work with the vacuum to get it clean (Fig 82). You may also find that the carpet will have dirty marks or stains that you cannot remove with the vacuum cleaner alone, but don't worry about this for now, as I'll deal with this in chapter ten, along with any marks and stains on the seats.

Once the boot/trunk area is clean,

Fig 83. Vacuum around the gearlever gaitor.

Fig 84. Make sure you get the crevice tool into the pockets behind the seats.

we can continue around to the other side of the car, and vacuum the other rear seat, underneath the seat pad, behind the seat's back rest, and the footwell – not forgetting those sculpted seat creases. Finally, we vacuum the last seat and footwell, including beneath and beside the seat.

There are a few more areas that will need the attention of the vacuum cleaner: the glove compartment, the centre console storage areas, ash tray (if fitted), and around the gearlever/shift and its gator or sleeve, which tends to hold dirt and dust in abundance (Fig 83). Make sure you don't forget the seat pockets (Fig 84) if you have them, and the door handle recesses and storage pockets (Fig 85) ... oh, and don't forget the parcel shelf if you have one! (Fig 86)

When you are happy with the vacuuming (Fig 87) we can then move on to the next task.

Fig 85. Clean the door handles.

Fig 86. Vacuum the parcel shelf.

Fig 87. The finished interior.

nine
Taking care of a leather interior

A leather interior is a touch of luxury in any car, and keeping it clean and in tip-top condition takes a little extra care and some special cleaning products. There are actually only two that you'll need: a leather cleaner, and a leather care cream or balm (Fig 88).

A good quality leather cleaner contains specialised cleaning agents that will safely clean and freshen your car's leather upholstery, and other interior leather surfaces, such as door panels, dash, and centre consoles.

You should **never** use household cleaners or detergents, as these are far too harsh to be used on leather. Specialised cleaners have a neutral pH balance to protect the leather from losing its essential oils during cleaning. These essential oils keep the leather supple and free from surface cracks. Once you've cleaned the leather, it should have a leather care cream or balm applied, to preserve and protect

Fig 88. Leather cleaner and balm/cream.

Fig 89. Test a small, inconspicuous area first.

Fig 90. Spray cleaner directly onto leather.

Fig 91. Wipe over with a soft cloth.

Fig 92. Rub leather with a cloth to remove dirt.

it. Leather is a natural material and if left unprotected and without nourishment, it will eventually dry out, become hard and brittle, and then crack.

Before cleaning your leather, it's important to test a small inconspicuous area with the cleaner, to ensure it's colour fast (Fig 89). Then, starting with the head rests and working your way down the seats, spray the cleaner directly onto the leather (Fig 90), before wiping over with a soft cotton cloth to remove the dirt (Figs 91 & 92). If there are any stubborn areas, you can agitate the cleaner with a small sponge, which should remove any remaining dirt.

Don't forget the door handles, as these can get very grubby (Fig 93), as too can the door pockets, which are prone to being kicked and scuffed as we enter and exit our car (Fig 94). A quick spray with cleaner (Fig 95) and a rub with the cloth will usually remove these scuff marks (Fig 96).

When all the leather has been cleaned, including door panels etc,

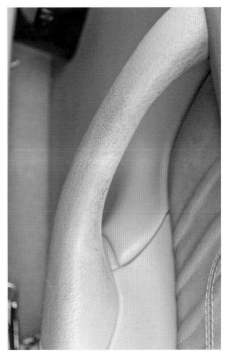

Fig 93. Check door handles for dirt.

Fig 94. Check for scuff marks.

Fig 95. Spray scuffs with cleaner.

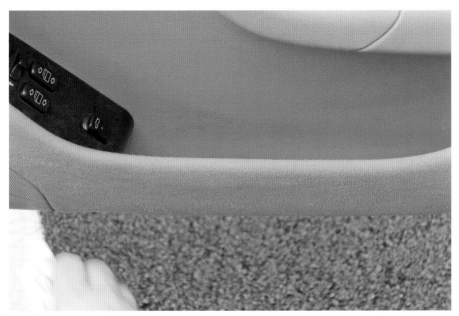

Fig 96. A quick wipe and it's gone.

you must apply the leather care cream or balm. Squeeze a small amount (about the size of a 5 pence/Dime) onto a soft cotton cloth (Fig 97), and apply to the leather, gently spreading and massaging it into the surface.

Make sure you give a good even coat to all the leather (Fig 98). This will nourish, moisturise, and help protect the leather from soiling and staining. Used regularly, it will preserve the natural look and feel of the leather, and make it easier to clean in future, too.

Finally, make sure that you never apply the cream or balm to leather that has not first been cleaned.

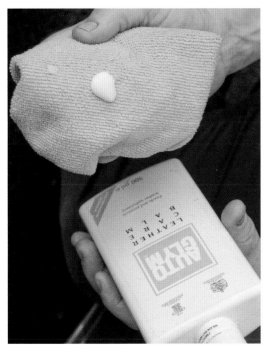

Fig 97. Apply leather balm/cream with a cloth.

Fig 98. Gently massage the balm/cream into the leather.

ten

Caring for your car's interior surfaces

Taking care of the interior surfaces of your car is pretty straightforward. Modern interiors are made from man-made materials, such as plastic and vinyl, but some are finished with natural materials like leather or wood. Whichever your car has, they all attract dust, and when you clean your car you'll need to give them a wipe with a soft cloth.

Sticky marks and dirt
If you find dirty or sticky marks, you'll need to use an interior cleaner or shampoo (Fig 99), that can either be sprayed directly onto the surface (Fig 100) to be cleaned, or onto a cloth.

Door handles are a common area for becoming grubby (Fig 101) and will need a regular wipe over with the shampoo. Sun visors and the edges and handles of glove compartments will also need regular attention.

Fig 99. Spray-on interior shampoo.

65

Fig 100. Spray directly onto surface to be cleaned.

Fig 101. Door handles become grubby.

Fig 102. Small stains can be easily removed.

Stains

You may have a stain from a spillage, or sticky marks from discarded sweets on your seats (Fig 102): interior shampoo will also tackle these.

Removing a small stain is quite straightforward: simply spray the stain with the interior shampoo (Fig 103); rub over with a clean cloth (Fig 104), and that should be enough to remove the stain (Fig 105). If it doesn't remove all of

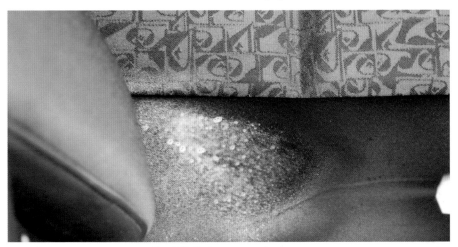

Fig 103. First, spray on shampoo.

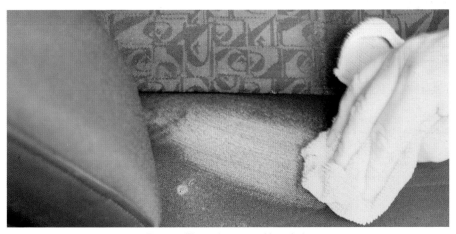

Fig 104. Then wipe over with a cloth.

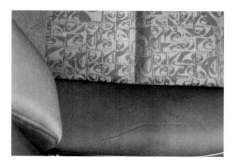

Fig 105. No more stain.

Fig 106. If you're cleaning a larger stain, regularly rinse your cloth with clean fresh water.

the stain the first time, simply repeat the process.

If you're cleaning a larger area with shampoo (a complete seat pad for instance), you should give the cloth a regular rinse in some clean fresh water (Fig 106) while cleaning.

Vinyl and plastic

When you've wiped over your surfaces with the shampoo, leave them to dry for a few minutes. Whilst they're drying you can clean the air vents with a paint brush, or the corner of a soft cloth, to remove any dust. You'll probably find other areas where dust collects, and these will also need the paint brush or cloth to clean them.

Once you are happy that you've removed all the dirt and dust, you can finish with either a non-silicone spray or a vinyl care spray (Fig 107). If you're using a non-silicone spray, give the surfaces a good buff with a clean soft cloth afterwards, to remove any build-up of the spray. If you leave excess spray on the surfaces, it will become sticky and attract more dust very quickly.

The vinyl care spray is easier to use if sprayed onto the cloth first, and also less messy, as you can apply it exactly where you need it (Fig 108). With both products, give them a good buff after applying, to remove any excess; this

Fig 107. Vinyl & Rubber Care spray gel.

will also leave a pleasant sheen, rather than a shine (Fig 109). A high-shine on the dash not only looks unnatural, but can cause reflections in the windscreen/windshield, which can be a dangerous distraction when driving.

If you have a leather interior, you'll probably have some leather trim throughout the rest of the car, too. Doors, for instance, may have a leather panel in them; you may have a leather covered steering wheel or gear change lever: if you didn't clean these when you cleaned the rest of your leather,

then take a clean soft cloth now, and wipe over with the leather cleaner (see chapter nine), to remove dirty marks. Once cleaned you can apply some leather cream/balm to feed and protect it from dirt and moisture.

Be sure to check the headlining for dirty marks, too, as this area often gets forgotten. Marks here are usually quickly and easily removed with the shampoo. Now your interior is finished, we're almost done – just a few finishing touches in the next chapter.

Fig 108. Spray cleaner directly onto the cloth for less mess.

Fig 109. Clean and fresh – just how it *should* look.

eleven
Finishing touches

In this chapter I'll be giving you a few tips on some of the finishing touches that will help to enhance the overall appearance of your car. I'll also make a few suggestions on some optional products that you may wish to consider purchasing, both to help protect the surfaces of your car and, as an added benefit, to make the task of keeping it clean somewhat easier in future.

Post-cleaning checks

Now that you've finished cleaning your car, it's usually a good idea to have a walk around it, just to make sure that you haven't missed anything, particularly if you've had to work in bad weather. You'll also need to have a good look around the interior, as this is where you'll have had the least amount of light to work by.

To begin with, check the seats and carpets to make sure that you didn't miss dirt or grit with the vacuum cleaner. Check the interior surfaces for missed dust, and check the windows, too.

Outside the car, have you buffed all of the polish? It's easy to miss some, especially on white or light-coloured paintwork. Next, check the windows for smears or insect remains, or stubborn bird mess that was not removed with the wash-off. A quick tip here: if you're struggling to remove insect remains or bird mess from windows, and all else fails, you can use a blade holder and blade to carefully scrape away the remains (Fig 110).

Now check around the door handles for missed polish, and the lips of the wheelarches for mud which, if left, can trap moisture and encourage corrosion. If your car has exterior vinyl trim that's looking a little faded, now is the time to apply some vinyl/rubber care gel. Just a little at a time, squeezed onto a piece of sponge is all you need

Fig 110. If all else fails, use a blade with a holder.

Fig 111. Just a small amount of gel is needed.

Fig 112. Rub over vinyl to freshen up.

Fig 113. Looks as good as new.

Fig 114. Spray the tyres evenly.

(Fig 111). Spread the gel gently over the trim (Fig 112) to give it a new-look sheen and revitalise some of the colour, making it look darker again (Fig 113).

Tyre dressing

After checking the wheels, you're almost done, with just the tyres to 'dress' for that finishing touch.

Using a spray-on tyre dressing, carefully spray around the tyre walls, avoiding the tyre treads and braking components.

Give them an even coating (Fig 114), and once coated, take a clean cloth and give the tyres a wipe to remove excess dressing and overspray from the wheel rims (Fig 115).

Fig 115. Wipe away excess from wheel rims and tyres.

Useful accessories

Some accessories available for the interior of your car will help to preserve its condition. For instance, if you're a dog owner you may want to consider buying a boot/trunk liner that will help protect it from dog hair and muddy paws. These are also great protection if you use your car for runs to the tip/refuse centre with household or garden waste.

Seat covers and mats
Two more very useful accessories are seat covers and rubber mats. If using seat covers, the waterproof variety is an excellent choice, as these not only help protect your seats from wet and muddy dogs, but also wet and muddy children – and for those inevitable accidents with drinks and sweets.

Rubber mats really will help to keep your carpets in tip-top condition, and they make vacuuming easier, too. If you don't like having rubber mats in your car, just use them during the winter months to give your carpets some extra protection during wet weather.

Air fresheners
An air freshener is another item you may want to consider. They come in many different forms (see page 12), but will last beyond a quick spray with an aerosol, keeping your car smelling fresh for a few weeks or more.

Protectors
Some final items you may want to consider are paint, glass, carpet and upholstery/leather protectors. There are many brands available, and they really can give lasting protection to your car's surfaces, making cleaning easier and more effective, and your car more attractive, all of which will help to preserve its re-sale value.

The end result

If you've followed the steps in this book, your car's exterior paintwork will have been treated with a protective coating that will enhance its natural lustre and provide a deep gloss. It will have had environmental and industrial contaminants removed effectively and safely, and it will be better protected against environmental contamination and industrial fallout in the future. It will have extra protection during severe winter weather, and all of your car's glass and mirrors will also have received a protective coating.

Carpets, upholstery, fabric or leather seats and door panels, etc, have been treated with a waterproof coating, sealing-out moisture and helping to protect them from staining. Accidental spills will just sit on the surface, enabling you to wipe them clean without it soaking in. Dust, dirt, and sticky marks will now be much easier to clean, too, as they won't penetrate the fabric or leather.

So, your car is now clean and looking its best for you to enjoy. Whilst this may have taken you a few hours to complete the first time, with practice you'll soon be achieving the same results in half the time!

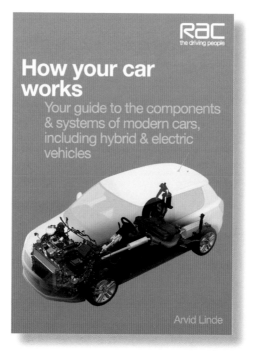

"Every car owner's little helper ... It's a book that could save you money, improve your knowledge of the car, and spur you on to bigger mechanical tasks."
The Daily Record

"An excellent and easy-to-understand introduction that answers many questions which some people may be afraid to ask."
MG Enthusiast

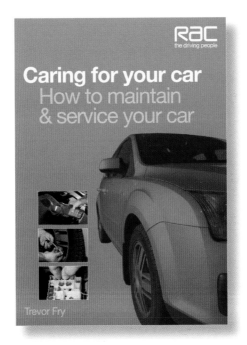

ISBN: 978-1-845843-96-0
• Paperback • 21x14.8cm • £9.99* UK/$19.95* USA
• 96 pages • 177 colour pictures

Also available in eBook format

For more info on Veloce titles, visit our website at www.veloce.co.uk
• email: info@veloce.co.uk • Tel: +44(0)1305 260068
* prices subject to change, p&p extra

ISBN: 978-1-845840-95-2
• Paperback • 21x14.8cm • £9.99* UK/$19.95* USA • 80 pages
• 101 colour pictures

Also available in eBook format

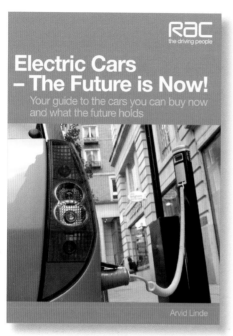

"Drivers with dogs will love this title ... directions are great ... the book deserves a place in any dog lovers' glovebox." *Auto Express*

"Approved by the RAC ... frequent motorway travellers should ensure they never leave the house without this guide." *Your Dog*

Get the App!

ISBN: 978-1-845841-02-7
• Paperback • 15x10.5cm
• £4.99* UK/$9.95* USA
• 208 pages • 200 colour pictures

Anyone who drives on the motorways will benefit from this guide to walks within 5 miles of motorway exits. Get more fun for your fuel, see more of the countryside, take a healthy break, or enjoy a relaxing lunch

Available on the iPhone
App Store

For more info on Veloce titles, visit our website at www.veloce.co.uk
• email: info@veloce.co.uk • Tel: +44(0)1305 260068
* prices subject to change, p&p extra

Index